21st Century Skills Library

GEOSCIENTIST

MATT MULLINS

Published in the United States of America by
Cherry Lake Publishing, Ann Arbor, Michigan
www.cherrylakepublishing.com

Content Adviser
Randall M. Richardson, PhD, Professor of Geosciences, University of Arizona,
Tucson, Arizona

Photo Credits: Cover and page 1, ©iStockphoto.com/gremlin; page 4, USGS/
Cascades Cascades Volcano Observatory, Dan Dzurisin; page 6, ©AP Photo/Jack
Smith; pages 8 and 12, ©Brian Lasenby/Dreamstime.com; pages 10, 15, and 18,
©Goodluz/Shutterstock, Inc.; page 14, ©Alexander Raths/Shutterstock, Inc.;
page 16, ©Radu Razvan/Shutterstock, Inc.; page 20, ©AP Photo/Daily Sentinel,
Dean Humphrey; page 21, ©zebrik/Shutterstock, Inc.; page 23, ©Lipik/Shutterstock,
Inc.; page 24, ©auremar/Shutterstock, Inc.; page 26, ©cubephoto/Shutterstock,
Inc.; page 27, ©Darren Baker/Shutterstock, Inc.

Library of Congress Cataloging-in-Publication Data
Mullins, Matt.
  Geoscientist/by Matt Mullins.
      p. cm.—(Cool STEM careers) (21st century skills library)
  Audience: Grades 4 to 6.
  Includes bibliographical references and index.
  ISBN 978-1-62431-004-1 (lib. bdg.) — ISBN 978-1-62431-028-7 (pbk.) —
ISBN 978-1-62431-052-2 (e-book)
 1. Earth sciences—Vocational guidance—Juvenile literature. 2. Earth scientists—
Juvenile literature. 3. Geology—Vocational guidance—Juvenile literature.
4. Geologists—Juvenile literature. I. Title.
  GB58.M85 2013
  550.23—dc23   2012034719

Cherry Lake Publishing would like to acknowledge
the work of The Partnership for 21st Century Skills.
Please visit *www.21stcenturyskills.org* for more information.

Printed in the United States of America
Corporate Graphics Inc.
January 2013
CLSP12

COOL STEM CAREERS

R0428524349

TABLE OF CONTENTS

GEOSCIENTIST

CHAPTER ONE
STUDYING THE EARTH

N eil awoke one Sunday morning in his home in Washington State and looked out the window. He couldn't believe what he saw. It looked like snow, but the date was May 18, 1980—and late spring was certainly *not* the season

The eruption of Mount St. Helens covered parts of the surrounding area in a thick layer of ash.

for it to be snowing in the Northwest. Yet everything outside Neil's window was covered in several inches of white stuff.

Neil rubbed his eyes and took a closer look. The stuff covering everything wasn't pure white—it was light gray. Whatever it was kept dropping from the sky, making the air look misty. Then Neil saw his father outside, walking through the falling stuff. He was in short sleeves and wearing a surgical mask. Neil's father, however, was not a doctor.

Neil realized what was falling and covering the ground: ash. Everywhere he looked, he saw volcanic ash. He soon learned that less than 40 miles (64 kilometers) away, Mount St. Helens had erupted. The volcano had blasted off most of its north side. The earth had quaked, and a column of ash from the explosion rose 15 miles (24 km) into the air in just 15 minutes! Most of the heavy, dark ash was blown north and east. Luckily, Neil's house was south and west!

■ ■ ■

On the day of the earthquake, winds carried away about 520 million tons (470 million metric tons) of ash. In Spokane, Washington, 250 miles (402 km) away, the air was so full of dark ash that it seemed like nighttime in the middle of the afternoon. The next day, people in Alberta, Canada, were scraping ash off their cars. They lived more than 600 miles (966 km) away from the volcano!

According to geoscientists, experts who study the earth, the eruption was the most damaging volcanic event in U.S. history. The mountain blew a cloud of steam, gas, rocks, and ash out its side at more than 300 miles an hour (483 km/hour). It knocked down 230 square miles (596 square km) of trees in three minutes. It also killed 57 people; thousands of deer, elk, and bears; and millions of fish.

When the quakes and eruptions settled, the mountain looked hollowed out. The blast had created a huge crater that

Fifty-seven people died in the May 1980 eruption.

opened to the north. The eruption was so powerful that it reduced the height of the mountain by 1,300 feet (396 meters).

This devastating event gave geoscientists an opportunity to study a volcanic eruption up close. Geoscientists study natural processes such as volcanic activity that are happening every moment. Because the earth has so much going on, there are many kinds of geoscientists. Each kind of geoscientist studies a particular natural process.

Geologists are geoscientists who study nature, the earth's history, and the materials and processes that shape our planet. They study layers of rock, canyons, caves, and **natural history**. Some focus on **glaciers**, some on underground oil reserves, and others on mining for metals.

Paleontologists study **fossils**. By looking at these remains and the impressions of plants and animals in solid rock, they try to determine the history of life on our planet. To learn about prehistoric animal behavior, some look for fossilized tracks made by animals that moved in large herds or traveled alone. Some focus on dinosaurs, while others look at the fossil remains of plants and simple life-forms.

Volcanologists study volcanoes. They investigate volcanoes and volcanic events to better understand their destructive powers and to predict future eruptions.

Other geoscientists, called meteorologists, study weather. These people look at gases and particles in our **atmosphere**. They also research weather events such as hurricanes and tornadoes. Meteorologists carefully investigate our planet's **climate** to determine how and why it changes.

Their research helps them forecast weather events, such as rainfall and snowfall, wind patterns, and temperature.

Hydrogeologists are geoscientists who study water. They study how water moves above and below the surface of the earth. They look at how minerals and things humans put in the ground, such as chemicals and waste, affect underground water. They also help find good places for wells to be built so that clean water can be taken from **groundwater** sources.

Some oceanographers get up close and personal with underwater life.

Oceanographers study the ocean floor, ocean currents, waves, sea life, and other aspects of ocean environments. These geoscientists explore how oceans formed and how the seas support life on the planet.

These are just some of the many fascinating careers in geoscience. Working as one type of geoscientist often requires knowledge about other geosciences. The geosciences are as connected as the different parts of nature! Geoscientists draw all that knowledge together to help us better understand and care for our home—planet Earth!

LEARNING & INNOVATION SKILLS

Have you ever thought of continents on the globe as puzzle pieces? In the early 1900s, German geologist and meteorologist Alfred Wegener published his idea that the continents were once one big supercontinent. Over time, this huge landmass broke apart, and the continents drifted. Wegener devoted years to proving his theory, but he died in 1930 while doing research in Greenland. In the 1960s, geoscientists proved Wegener right by discovering that the earth's outer layer is made of giant plates of rock that move over a weaker, partially melted layer of rock. At one time, the continents *were* all one big landmass!

CHAPTER TWO
WORKING AS A GEOSCIENTIST

R andy is a hydrogeologist who works for the United States Geological Survey (USGS). The USGS is an organization that studies America's environment and natural

Geoscientists use computers to do research and perform tests.

resources. It also examines the impact of climate change, how we use the land, and what natural hazards threaten us.

Randy starts his workday at home by checking his e-mail. People from all over the world send him questions about groundwater. Randy replies to each one. Then he looks at computer **models** of groundwater **reservoirs** around the world. Randy checks surface water supplies, too. He searches for places where an event such as an earthquake or an accident might have harmed that region's water supplies.

After finishing these important tasks, he showers, eats breakfast, hops on his bicycle, and pedals to work. Randy spends the first part of his day with his research team. The USGS helps cities, states, and companies with water-related problems. It has many projects going on at once. Randy talks with the team about their projects.

For example, the state of Wisconsin had approached the USGS with an important concern. Northern Wisconsin has many lakes. Birds called loons live near many of these lakes. Some businesspeople wanted to build homes and offices in the region. Meanwhile, the earth's climate is changing. Wisconsin officials wanted to know what would happen to the loon **habitat** when buildings and streets were constructed. They also wanted to determine how changes in the region's average temperature and rainfall would affect the loons. Even if they change just a little, could that harm the loons?

To find the answers, Randy and his team run computer models. They use different climate change possibilities that other scientists provide. They run their water models to see how each possibility will affect the loons. They also change their models to include the streets and buildings that are being planned. The team predicts how loons will react to each situation.

Geoscientists work to protect the environment so wild animals such as loons have room to live and grow.

Later, Randy talks with some Wisconsin officials. He tells state workers what progress his team is making on their project. He updates city officials on their water supply projects. Randy explains to an environmental group the steps remaining in the USGS's research on its question.

LEARNING & INNOVATION SKILLS

Geoscientists rely on computers for a lot of their work. Sometimes, the computer models that geoscientists run show very slow processes, such as the movement of continents or the movement of **magma** beneath the earth's crust. Other times, models can give glimpses of things we cannot see, such as the superhot metal of the earth's core. Hydrogeologists use modeling to show how water seeps into soil and eventually collects in groundwater reservoirs. Do you enjoy computers? If so, you may one day create new computer models to use in geoscience.

Randy often speaks to the public about his job. He visits elementary schools, where he shares with students the ins and outs of his workday. He attends meetings to discuss water issues with the public and city officials. He also teaches a college class. Once in a while, Randy gets to do one of his favorite things: work outside! He works with officials and engineers to help cities dig wells. Sometimes, he measures how much water flows in a stream. He may also study how water seeps through the ground to help refill an underground reservoir.

Scientists often share their knowledge by teaching classes.

A geoscientist might bring students into the field so they can get a close look at what it's like to perform research in natural environments.

Jean is a professor of hydrogeology at the University of Wisconsin–Madison. Like Randy, she starts the day at her computer. She reviews the teaching notes and lesson plans she's made for the day's classes. After that, Jean goes to school and teaches her classes in the morning. Then she goes to work in her office, where she answers e-mail and

Keeping up-to-date with the latest scientific ideas can be time consuming.

reads scientific articles and online updates about the latest developments in hydrogeology.

Jean was president of the Geological Society of America (GSA) from 2009 to 2010. The GSA helps geoscientists share research and advises them how to work with governments around the world. More than 24,000 people in more than 100 countries are members of this organization, which was founded in 1888. GSA members identify the ideas and concerns in geoscience that require the attention of governments and people.

Jean stays in close contact with the GSA even though she is no longer its president. These days, she mainly works with her students. She meets with them to discuss the material she's teaching and to help them with the research they are doing.

Jean often meets with other professors. They discuss issues about geoscience and share ideas about how to improve the teaching of it. Despite the classes, meetings, and other work, Jean makes time to attend scientific meetings. As a professor and a scientist who does research, she wants to stay informed about what other geoscientists are doing.

Like Randy, who was once Jean's student, Jean likes to work outdoors. She enjoys observing water flow and studying plants and rocks that provide clues about groundwater. She also enjoys studying the way pollution can get into groundwater.

CHAPTER THREE
BECOMING A GEOSCIENTIST

Do you enjoy being outside? If you like camping or hiking, you might enjoy the work of a geoscientist. Of course, geoscience isn't just about playing in the dirt!

Plants have a powerful effect on the air, soil, and water around them.

It takes years to become a geoscientist. Like many other scientists, geoscientists have to possess sharp math skills. They also have to study biology, chemistry, and physics. Biology is the study of life. As Randy says, "I would have taken more biology. Plants, fungus, and trees tell us a lot about the water they draw from." Chemistry focuses on the ways in which material is structured and interacts with other materials. Physics concerns the ways in which things act on one another. It focuses on physical forces, such as gravity.

LIFE & CAREER SKILLS

Scientists read scientific journals for the latest and most accurate scientific information. Jean, Randy, and other scientists write articles about their research. They submit these articles to journals. The journal editor sends the article to other scientists who review it. The reviewers comment on the article, ask questions about it, and suggest changes, if necessary. If the author makes the requested changes, the journal may publish the article. Not all articles, however, are accepted for publication. This process ensures that the scientific information is accurate and reflects the latest knowledge.

Once in college, future geoscientists have to take geoscience courses and more advanced classes in—you guessed it—math, biology, chemistry and physics! Some geoscientist jobs, however, don't require many years of college study. For example, **petroleum** technicians support scientists and engineers in the search for minerals, oil, and natural gas. These assistant scientists can get jobs with a two-year degree or special training after high school.

Petroleum technicians help prevent oil and gas wells from polluting the environment.

Chemistry classes are an important part of a geoscientist's education.

Most jobs in the geosciences, however, require more education. A four-year college degree is a strong start. Many geoscientists also get graduate degrees—a master's or a doctorate degree.

Hydrologists often have master's degrees. These scientists study water supply and water quality, and make sure we get clean water into our homes. It's not unusual to find a hydrologist with a master's degree working with a geoscientist who has a doctorate degree. Randy has a doctorate. Many members of his team have graduate degrees. Jean also has a doctorate degree. It's very difficult to get a job as a professor without one—and some professors even have more than one!

It's important for geoscientists to have strong writing and speaking skills. Jean and Randy both write scientific papers. They speak before groups of geoscientists, the public, students, and government officials. Speaking and writing require strong language skills. So if you want to go far, make sure you take plenty of English classes and writing instruction.

Geoscientists such as Randy often work with people who aren't geoscientists. Randy frequently works with engineers, businesspeople, and government officials. Randy says it's becoming more common for him to work with people from many different areas of expertise.

Working and communicating with others is an important part of being a geoscientist.

CHAPTER FOUR

GEOSCIENCE IN THE FUTURE

The future for people working in the field of geoscience looks bright. According to the U.S. government, geoscience will

Geoscience will be an especially important field in the years to come.

be adding jobs in the coming years. In fact, the outlook is that the number of jobs in geoscience will grow faster than in many other fields.

Some fields in geoscience are certain to grow. Hydrogeology is one. Many of the world's largest cities will be facing shortages of fresh, clean water in the future. In addition, safe drinking water makes up only about 1 percent of all the water on the planet. Dedicated hydrogeologists will be needed to find reliable new sources of fresh groundwater. Hydrogeologists will also be needed to study how to keep the groundwater we have clean and safe from pollution.

Geologists will play important roles in the future of humanity. The world's population will soon reach 9 billion people. These people will need energy to power their homes and businesses. They will need minerals and other natural resources for building and manufacturing. This huge global population will require many skilled geoscientists to find the natural resources that societies need.

Meteorologists and climate scientists are other geoscientists the world will continue to turn to for help. Our planet's climate is changing. Average temperatures are warmer than in the past, rainfall patterns are shifting, and sea levels are rising. As these changes continue, geoscientists will be counted on to offer solutions and predict future weather patterns that might affect people around the globe.

Fortunately, many geoscientists are meeting these challenges head-on. An increasing number of experts are getting involved in issues such as ocean health and resource management.

We can also expect that geoscientists will have better tools to use in their work. Computer technology advances by leaps and bounds each year. Improved wireless technology and

Some geoscientists work to ensure that people, plants, and animals have the clean water they need to live.

Computers provide geoscientists with new advantages in the fight to protect our planet.

satellites provide us with more accurate tools for searching both above the ground and below it.

People face constant change in the natural world. Geoscientists know that the earth has been changing for 4.6 billion years. They have made the earth, its resources, and its changes their life's work. As the planet changes and humans must adapt to these shifts, geoscientists will point the way ahead!

Are you up to the challenge of training to be a geoscientist?

21ST CENTURY CONTENT

Many scientists who study the planets are geoscientists. Planetary geologists study other planets the way geologists study Earth. Geomorphologists study quakes, meteor impacts, volcanoes, hydrology, and other processes that have shaped distant planets. Can you think of other areas of geoscience that might be applied to other planets?

SOME WELL-KNOWN GEOSCIENTISTS

Tanya Atwater (1942–) is a retired marine geologist. She used computer animation to show how the earth's plates interact. She also dove to the bottom of the ocean 12 times in a tiny underwater craft. Atwater focused on how the San Andreas Fault in California evolved, and she is devoted to informing the public about science issues.

Charles Darwin (1809–1882) may be known as the father of evolution, but he was also a skilled geologist. He collected fossils on his travels.

Harry Hess (1906–1969) mapped the landscape of the seafloor while in the U.S. Navy during World War II (1939–1945). He developed the idea that magma seeps up from deep within the earth in cracks on the seafloor.

M. King Hubbert (1903–1989) was a geologist who applied mathematics to the study of water flow. He later worked in petroleum geology. In 1956, he presented a theory claiming that the U.S. oil industry would reach peak production in the 1970s. Hubbert's peak oil theory has been very useful. He promoted nuclear and solar power as the most promising long-term energy sources.

O. E. Meinzer (1876–1948) is known as the father of hydrogeology. He showed how water flows over great distances through rock. Meinzer was a leader in finding groundwater sources and led the USGS Ground Water Division for more than 30 years.

Harrison Schmitt (1935–) was a geologist, professor, and astronaut. In 1972, he was one of the last two astronauts to walk on the moon. He was a U.S. senator representing New Mexico from 1976 to 1982 and worked for many years with the National Aeronautics and Space Administration (NASA).

GLOSSARY

atmosphere (AT-muhs-feer) the mixture of gases that surrounds a planet

climate (KLYE-mit) the weather typical of a place over a long period of time

fossils (FAH-suhlz) bones, shells, or other traces of an animal or plant from millions of years ago, preserved as rock

glaciers (GLAY-shurz) slow-moving masses of ice found on mountains or in polar regions

groundwater (GROUND-wah-tur) water far below the ground that can be used for drinking and other purposes

habitat (HAB-uh-tat) the place where an animal or a plant naturally lives

magma (MAG-muh) melted rock found beneath the earth's surface that becomes lava when it flows out of volcanoes

models (MAH-duhlz) mathematical or graphic representations of situations or natural events created with the help of a computer

natural history (NACH-ur-uhl his-TOR-ee) the study of living things and natural objects and happenings, and their origins and relationships

petroleum (puh-TROH-lee-uhm) a thick, oily liquid found below the earth's surface that is used to make gasoline, heating oil, and many other products

reservoirs (REZ-ur-vwahrz) natural or artificial lakes in which water is collected and stored for use

satellites (SAT-uh-lites) spacecraft that are sent into orbit around the earth, the moon, or another object in space, often used to track weather patterns or transmit communication signals

FOR MORE INFORMATION

BOOKS

Hartman, Eve, and Wendy Meshbesher. *Searching for Arctic Oil.* Chicago: Raintree, 2011.

Twist, Clint, Lisa Regan, and Camilla de la Bédoyère. *Extreme Earth.* Broomall, PA: Mason Crest Publishers, 2011.

Young, Greg. *Alfred Wegener: Pioneer of Plate Tectonics.* Minneapolis: Compass Point Books, 2009.

WEB SITES

American Geosciences Institute
www.youtube.com/agieducation
This site features videos about geoscience showing how humans change the earth, how life evolves on the earth, how the earth provides needed natural resources, and much more.

KidsGeo.com—Geology for Kids
www.kidsgeo.com/geology-for-kids
This site features dozens of articles about the earth, rocks, landforms, volcanoes, and much, much more.

INDEX

ABOUT THE AUTHOR

Matt Mullins holds a master's degree in the history of science from the University of Wisconsin–Madison. He writes about all kinds of things—science and technology, engineering, business, food, agriculture, and more. Matt has written more than 30 children's books and has made several short films. He lives in Madison, Wisconsin.

The author wishes to thank Randy Hunt of USGS and Jean Bahr of the University of Wisconsin–Madison for their help with this book.